VIOLA

Elementary Scales and Bowings

for STRINGS

by HARVEY S. WHISTLER and HERMAN A. HUMMEL

CONTENTS

RUBANK®

HAL•LEONARD® CORPORATION

7777 W. Bluemound Rd. P.O. Box 13819 Milwaukee, WI 53213

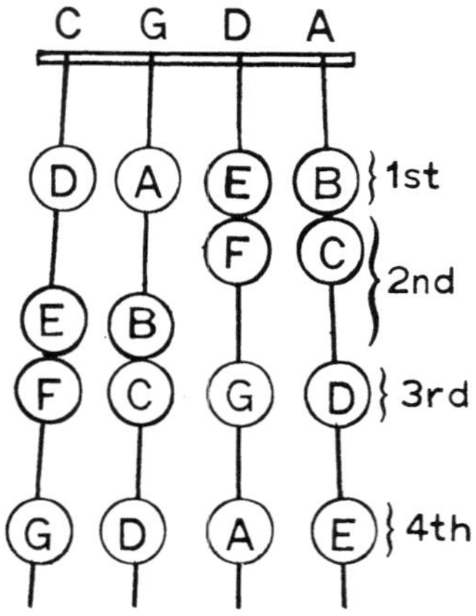

Key of C Major

Détaché Scale

1 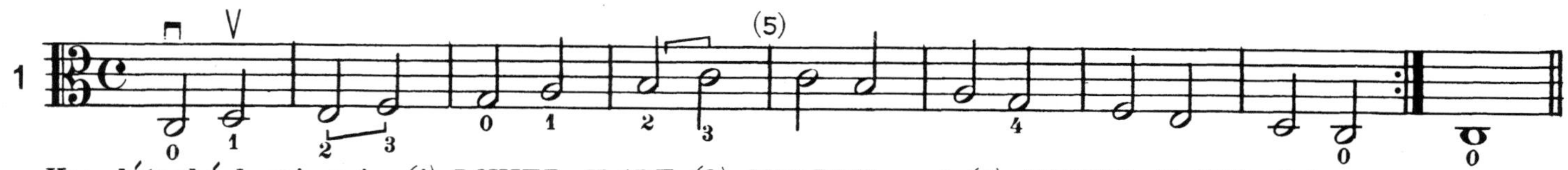

Use détaché bowing in (1) LOWER HALF, (2) MIDDLE, and (3) UPPER HALF of bow.

Slurred Scales

Legato (Smooth and connected)

2 

3 

4 

Detached Bowings

Broad and detached

5 

Staccato (Short and detached)

6 

Bow Division

7 

8 

Détaché Scale in Quarter Notes

9 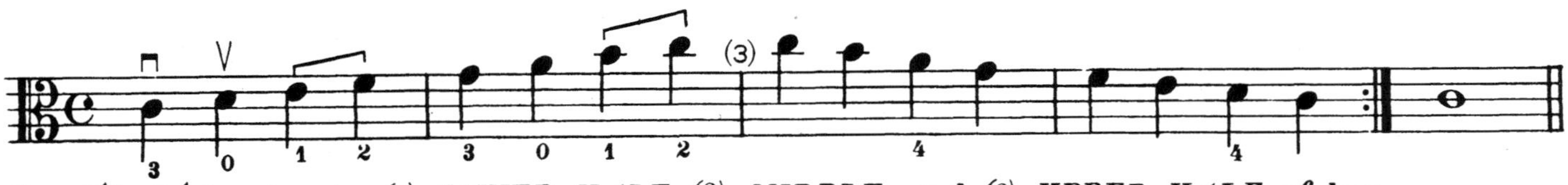

Use détaché bowing in (1) LOWER HALF, (2) MIDDLE, and (3) UPPER HALF of bow.

Broken Chords

10 

11 

Tone Study

12 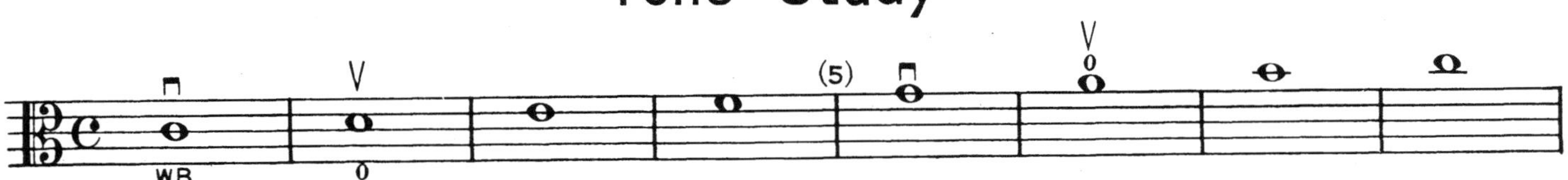

Also practice very slowly, sustaining each tone for EIGHT counts.

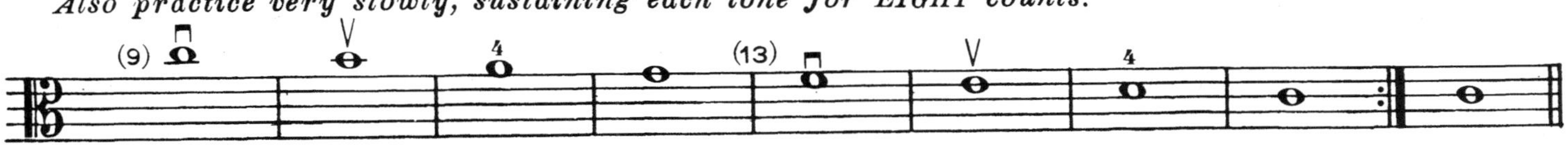

Eighth Notes

13 

Also practice (1) slurring each TWO notes, and (2) slurring each FOUR notes.

Quarter and Eighth Notes

14 

15 

16 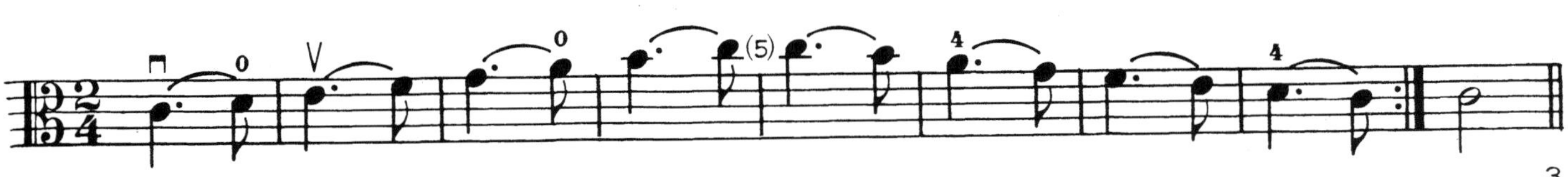

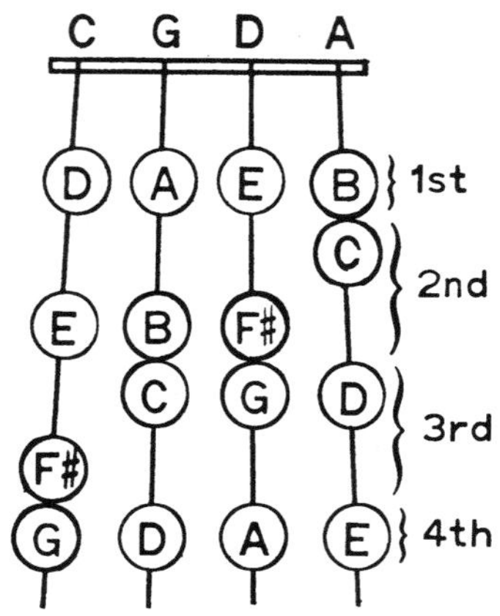

Key of G Major

Détaché Scale

17 

Use détaché bowing in (1) LOWER HALF, (2) MIDDLE, and (3) UPPER HALF of bow.

Slurred Scales

Legato (Smooth and connected)

18 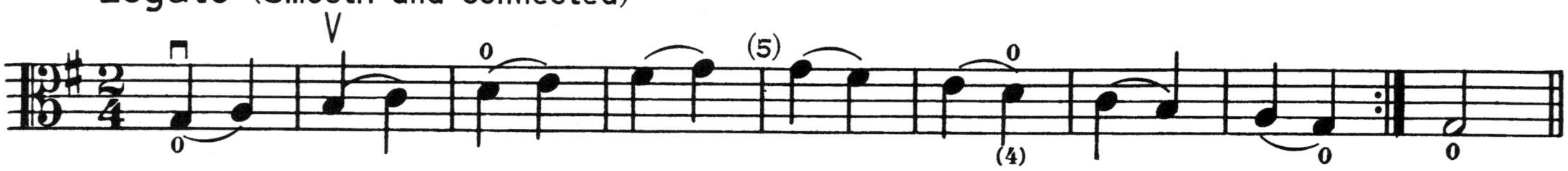

19 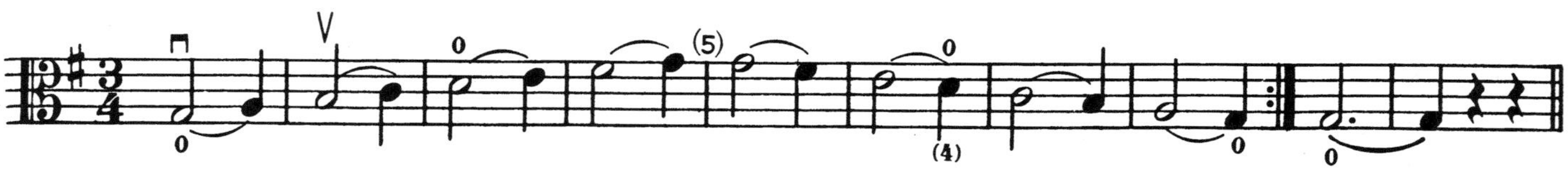

20 

Detached Bowings

Broad and detached

21 

Staccoto (Short and detached)

22 

Bow Division

23 

24 

Détaché Scale in Quarter Notes

25 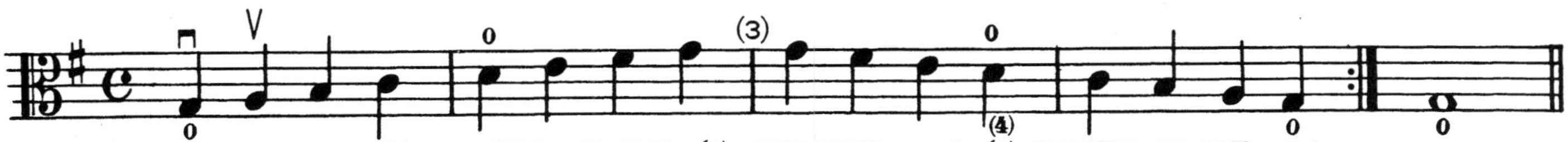

Use détaché bowing in (1) LOWER HALF, (2) MIDDLE, and (3) UPPER HALF of bow.

Broken Chords

26 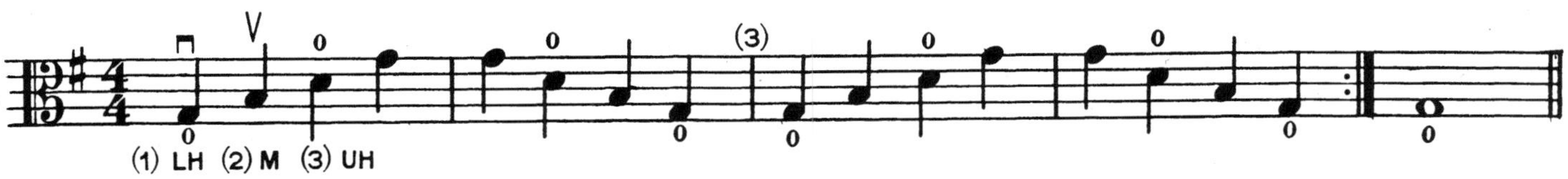

27 

Tone Study

28 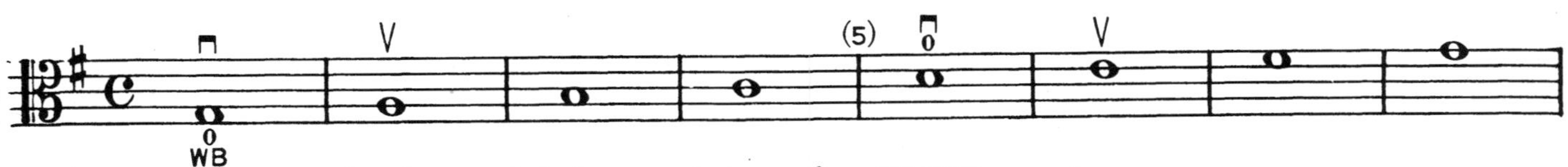

Also practice very slowly, sustaining each tone for EIGHT counts.

Eighth Notes

29 

Also practice (1) slurring each TWO notes, and (2) slurring each FOUR notes.

Quarter and Eighth Notes

30 

31 

32 

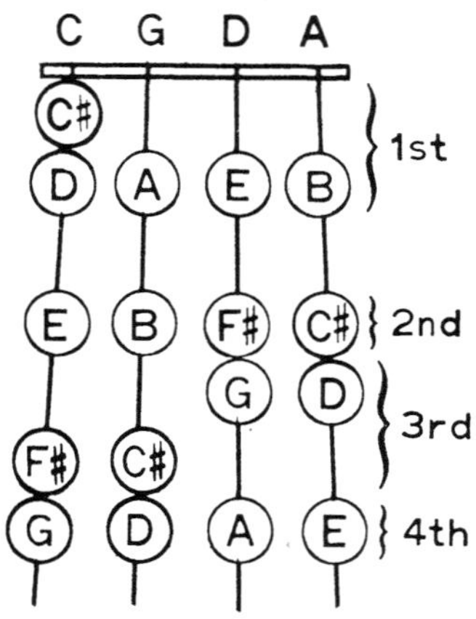

Key of D Major

Détaché Scale

33 

Use détaché bowing in (1) LOWER HALF, (2) MIDDLE, and (3) UPPER HALF of bow.

Slurred Scales

Legato (Smooth and connected)

34 

35 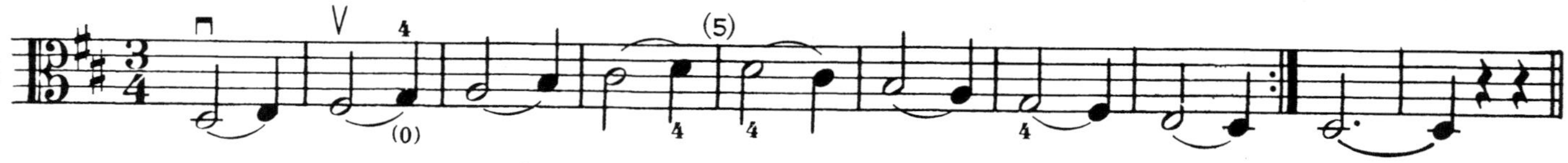

36 

Detached Bowings

Broad and detached

37 

Staccato (Short and detached)

38 

Bow Division

39 

40 

Détaché Scale in Quarter Notes

41 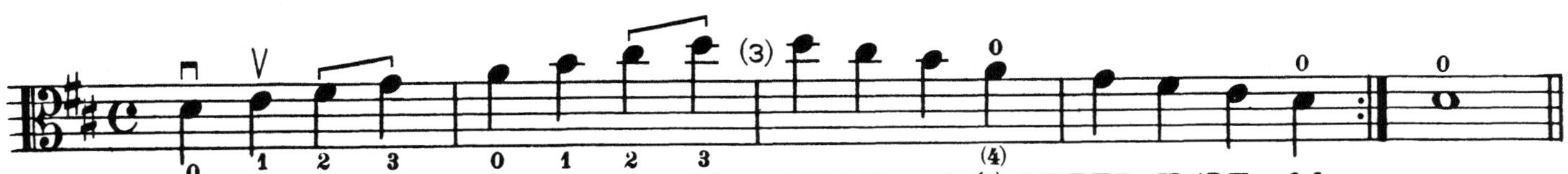

Use détaché bowing in (1) LOWER HALF, (2) MIDDLE, and (3) UPPER HALF of bow.

Broken Chords

42 

43 

Tone Study

44 

Also practice very slowly, sustaining each tone for EIGHT counts.

Eighth Notes

45 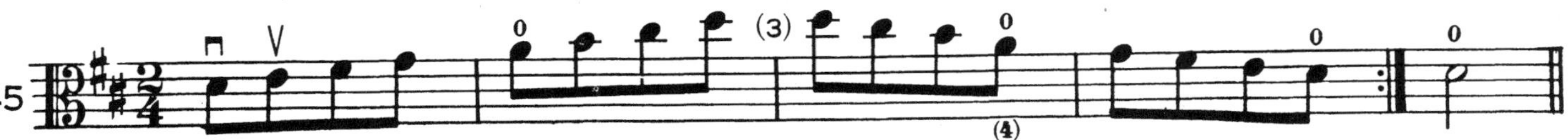

Also practice (1) slurring each TWO notes, and (2) slurring each FOUR notes.

Quarter and Eighth Notes

46 

47 

48 

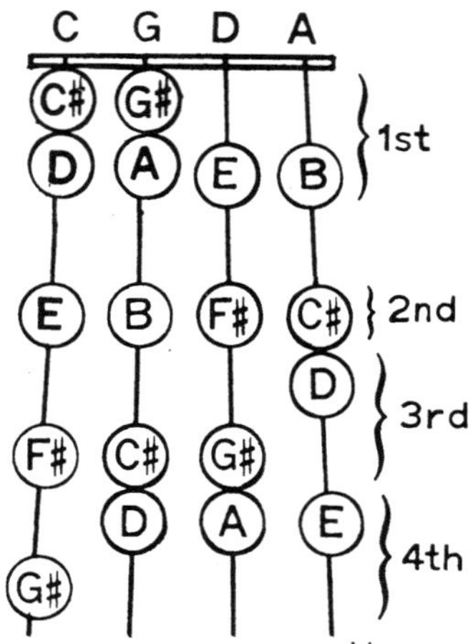

Key of A Major

Détaché Scale

49 

Use détaché bowing in (1) LOWER HALF, (2) MIDDLE, and (3) UPPER HALF of bow.

Slurred Scales

Legato (Smooth and connected)

50 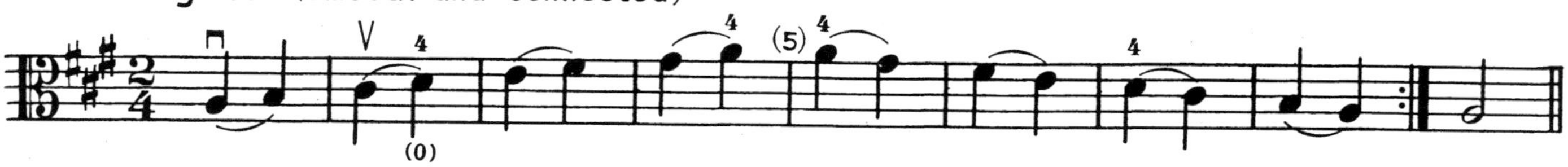

51 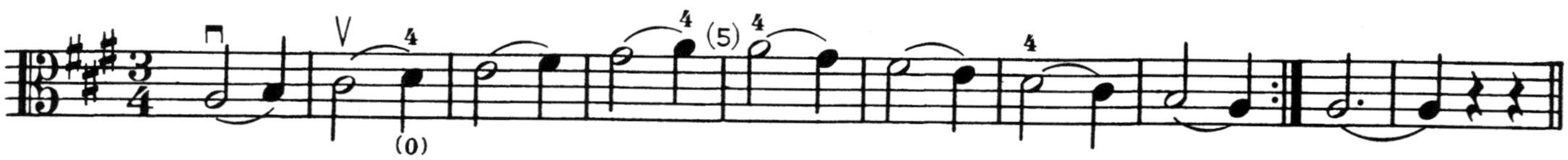

52 

Detached Bowings

Broad and detached

53 

Staccato (Short and detached)

54 

Bow Division

55 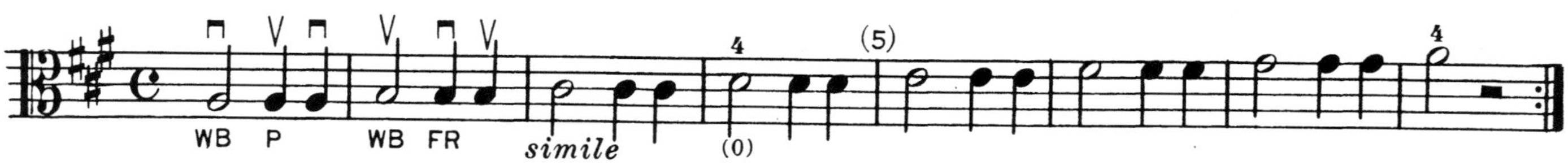

56 

Détaché Scale in Quarter Notes

57

Use détaché bowing in (1) LOWER HALF, (2) MIDDLE, and (3) UPPER HALF of bow.

Broken Chords

58

59

Tone Study

60
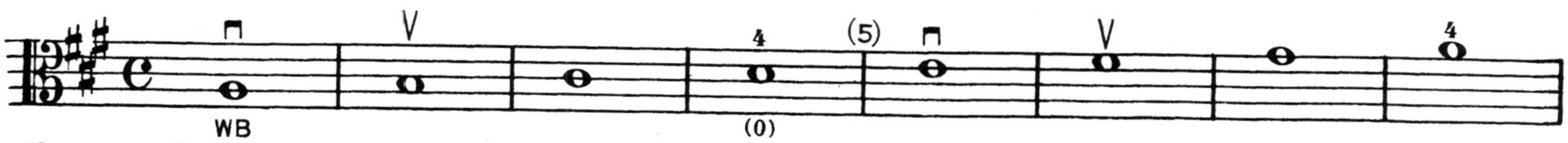

Also practice very slowly, sustaining each tone for EIGHT counts.

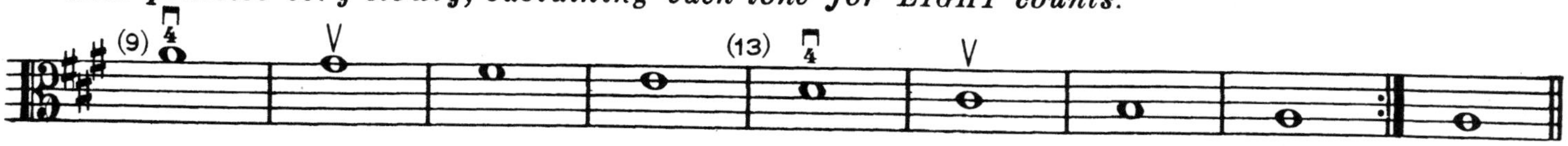

Eighth Notes

61

Also practice (1) slurring each TWO notes, and (2) slurring each FOUR notes.

Quarter and Eighth Notes

62
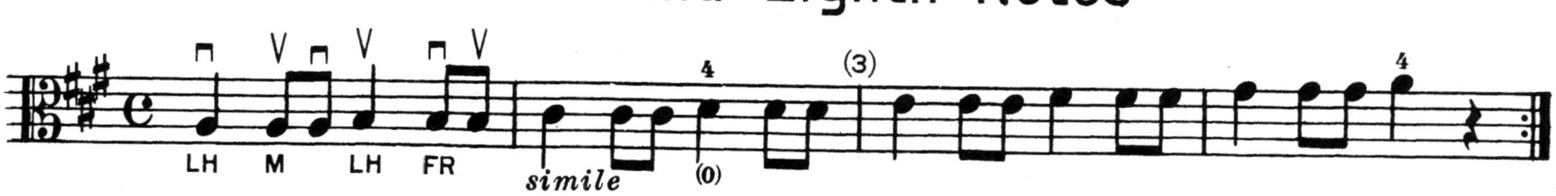

63

64

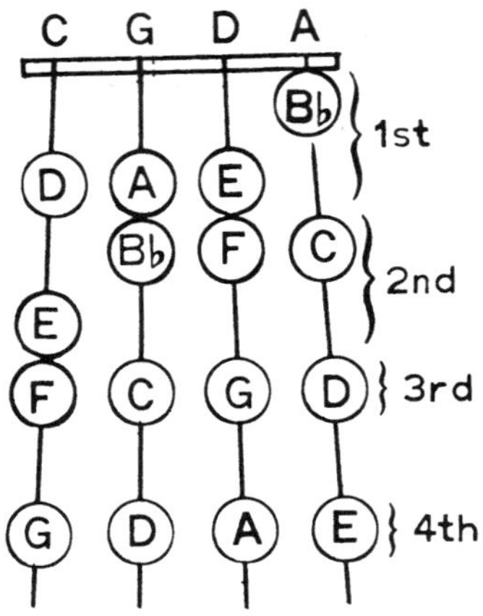

Key of F Major

Détaché Scale

65 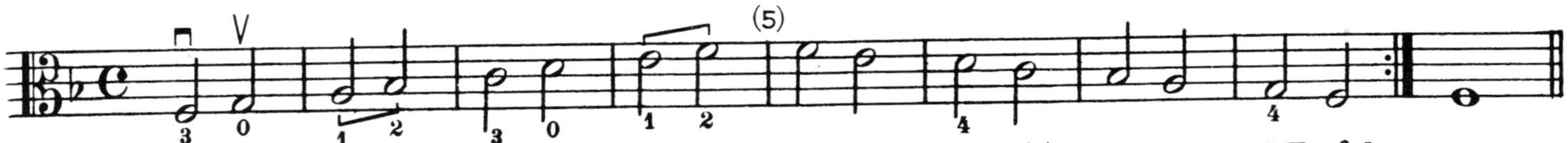

Use détaché bowing in (1) LOWER HALF, (2) MIDDLE, and (3) UPPER HALF of bow.

Slurred Scales

Legato (Smooth and connected)

66 

67 

68 

Detached Bowings

Broad and detached

69 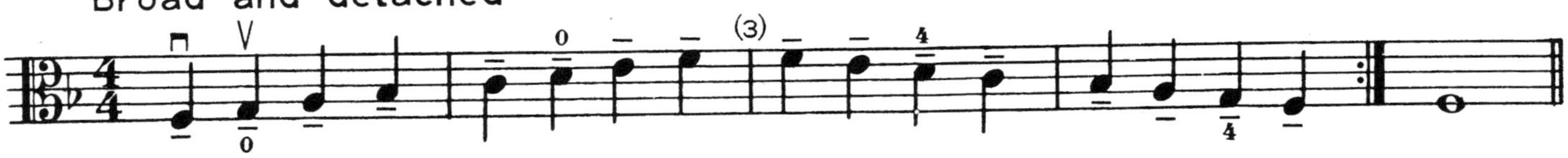

Staccato (Short and detached)

70 

Bow Division

71 

72 

Détaché Scale in Quarter Notes

73 

Use détaché bowing in (1) UPPER HALF, (2) MIDDLE, and (3) LOWER HALF of bow.

Broken Chords

74 

75 

Tone Study

76 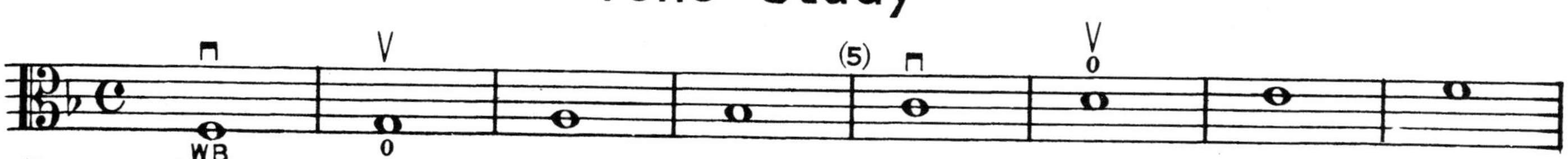

Also practice very slowly, sustaining each tone for EIGHT counts.

Eighth Notes

77 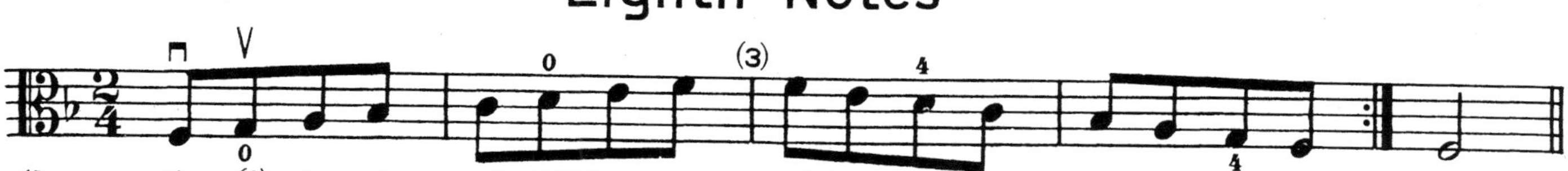

Also practice (1) slurring each TWO notes, and (2) slurring each FOUR notes.

Quarter and Eighth Notes

78 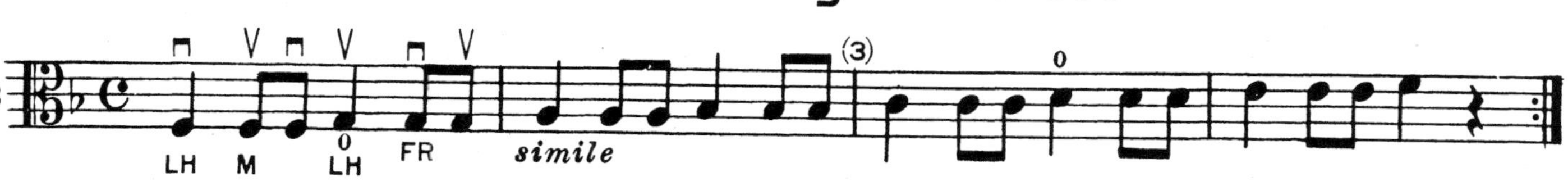

79 

80 

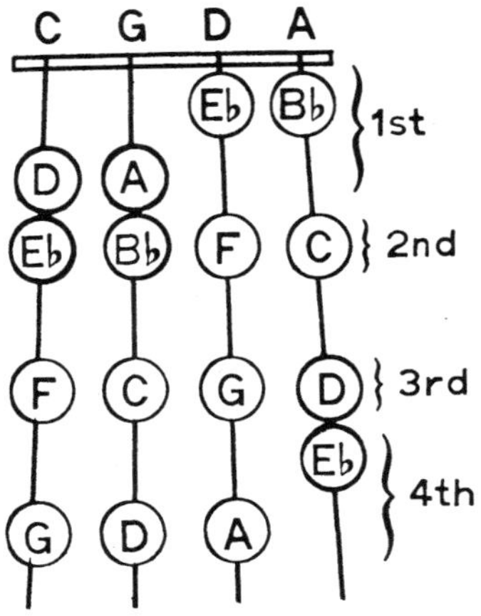

Key of B♭ Major

Détaché Scale

81 

Use détaché bowing in (1) LOWER HALF, (2) MIDDLE, and (3) UPPER HALF of bow.

Slurred Scales

Legato (Smooth and connected)

82 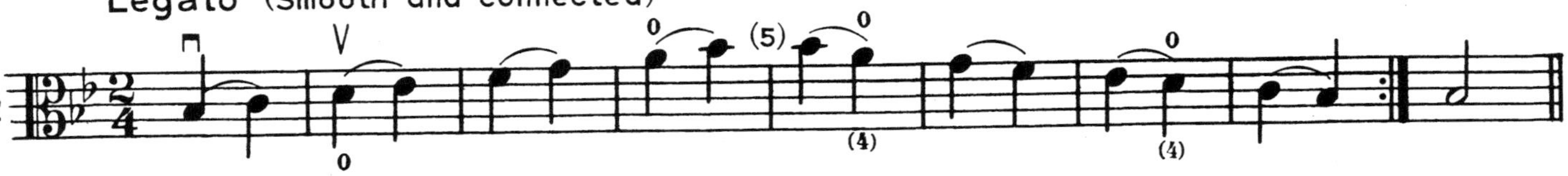

83 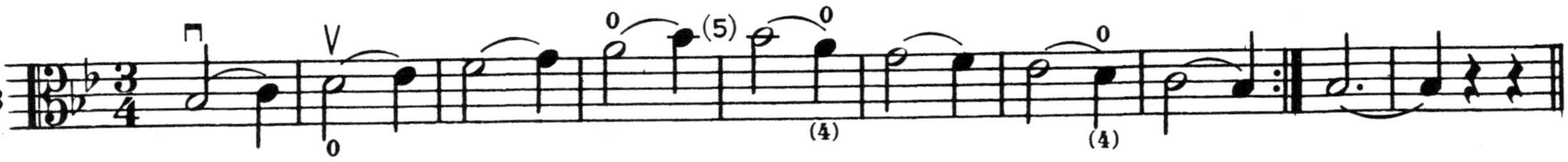

84 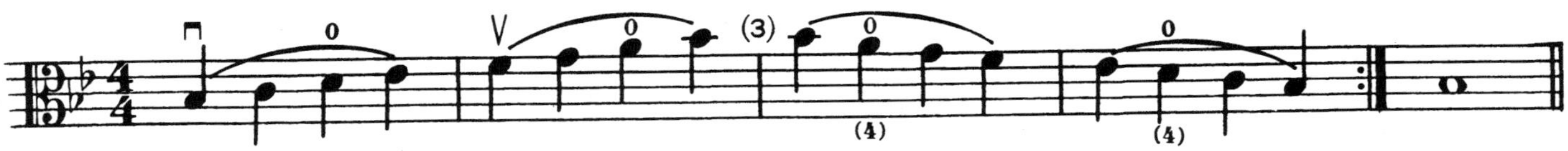

Detached Bowings

Broad and detached

85 

Staccato (Short and detached)

86 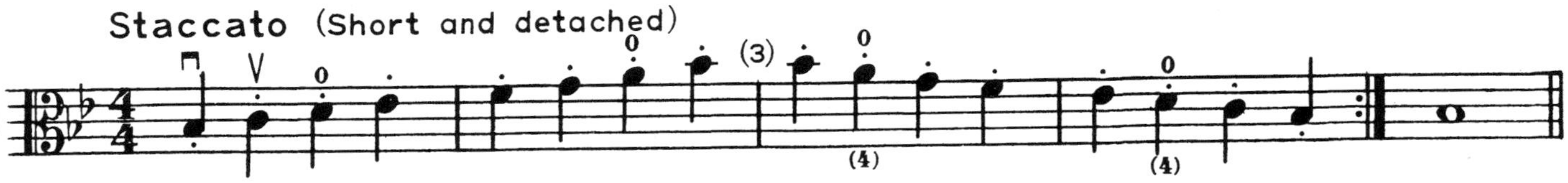

Bow Division

87 

88 

Détaché Scale in Quarter Notes

89 

Use détaché bowing in (1) LOWER HALF, (2) MIDDLE, and (3) UPPER HALF of bow.

Broken Chords

90 

91 

Tone Study

92 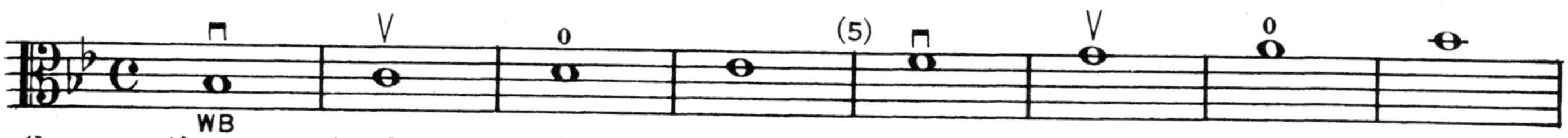

Also practice very slowly, sustaining each tone for EIGHT counts.

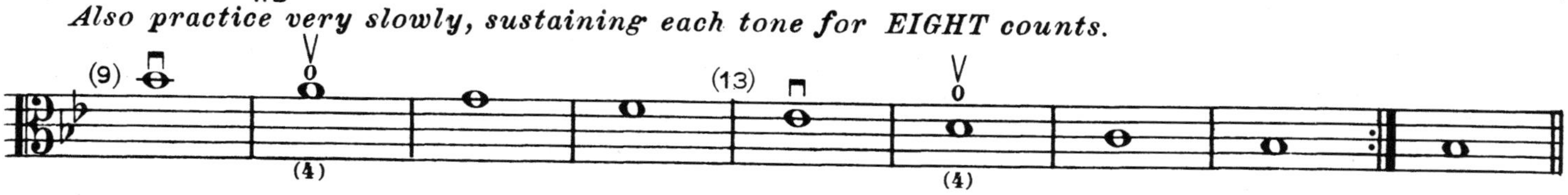

Eighth Notes

93 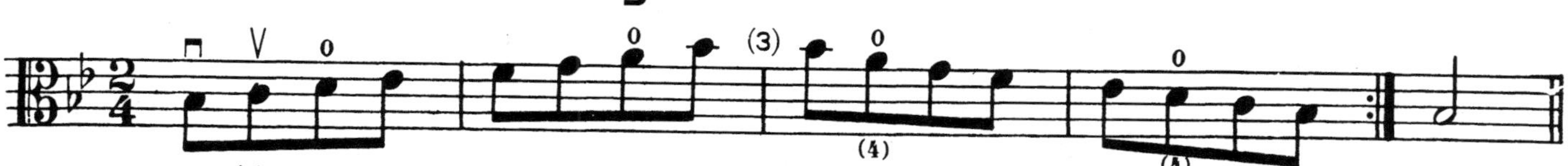

Also practice (1) slurring each TWO notes, and (2) slurring each FOUR notes.

Quarter and Eighth Notes

94 

95 

96 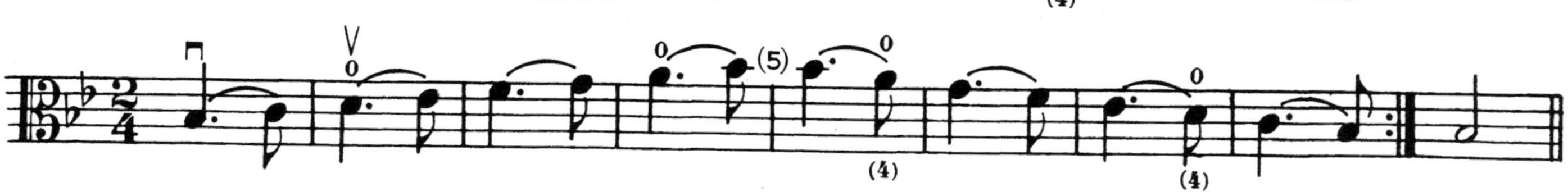

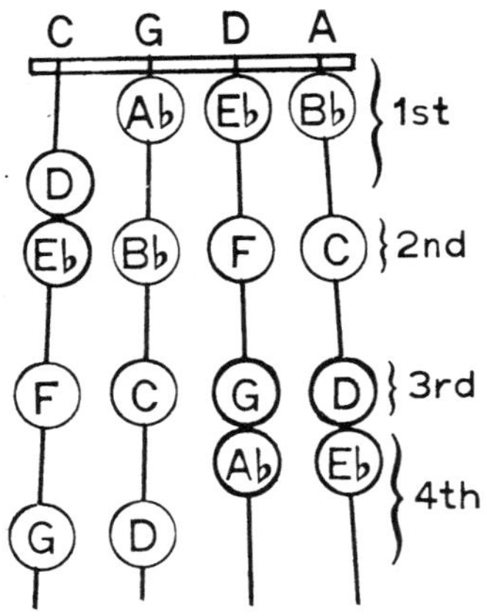

Key of E♭ Major

Détaché Scale

97 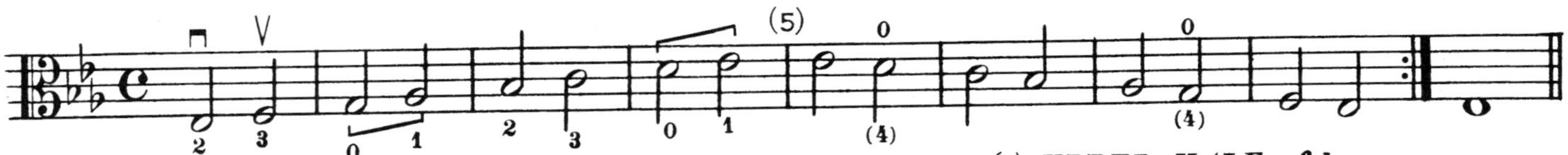

Use détaché bowing in (1) LOWER HALF, (2) MIDDLE, and (3) UPPER HALF of bow.

Slurred Scales

Legato (Smooth and connected)

98 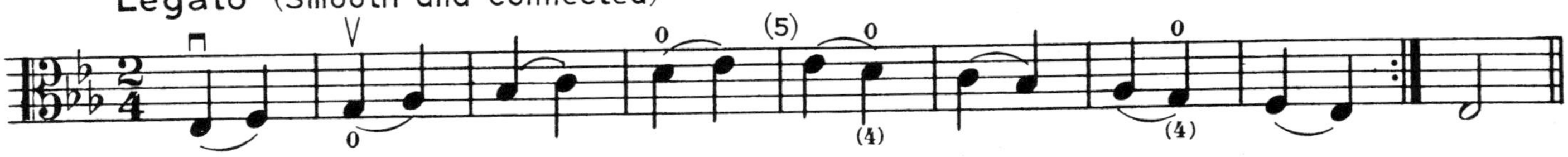

99 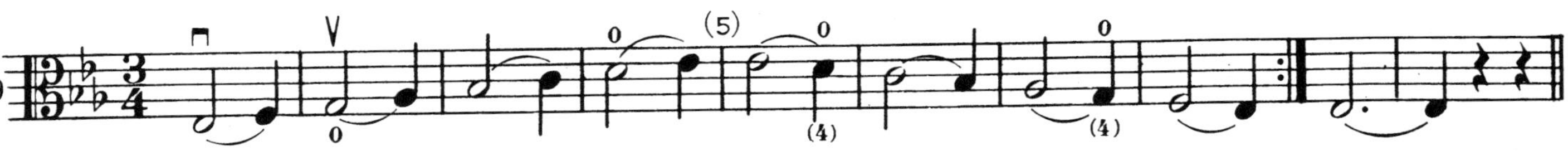

100 

Detached Bowings

Broad and detached

101 

Staccato (Short and detached)

102 

Bow Division

103 

104 

Détaché Scale in Quarter Notes

105 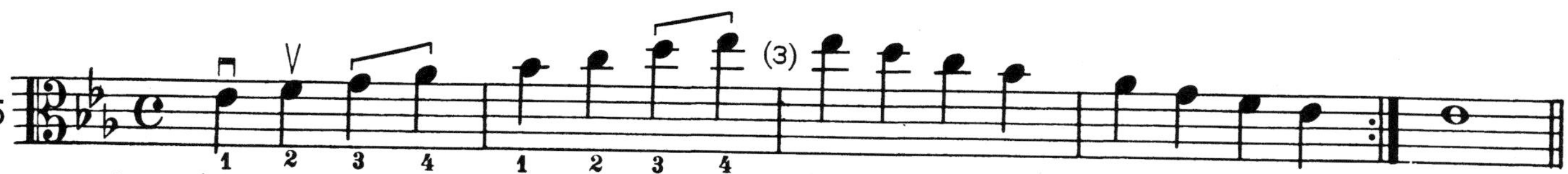

Use détaché bowing in (1) LOWER HALF, (2) MIDDLE, and (3) UPPER HALF of bow.

Broken Chords

106 

107 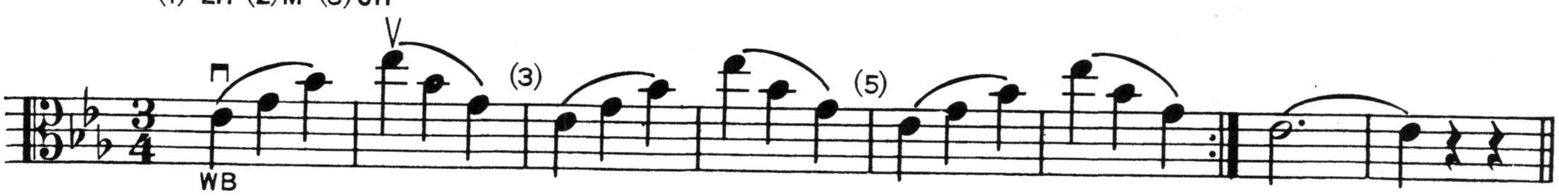

Tone Study

108 

Also practice very slowly, sustaining each tone for EIGHT counts.

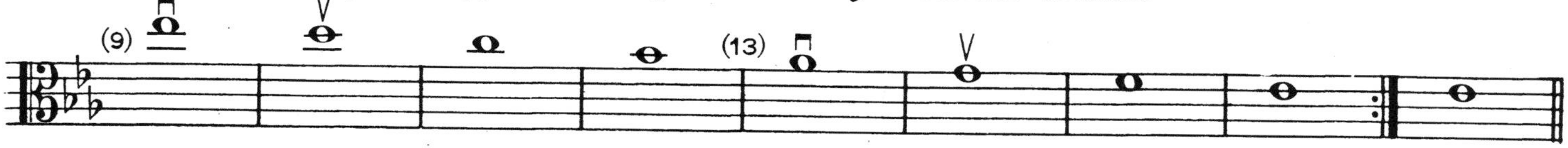

Eighth Notes

109 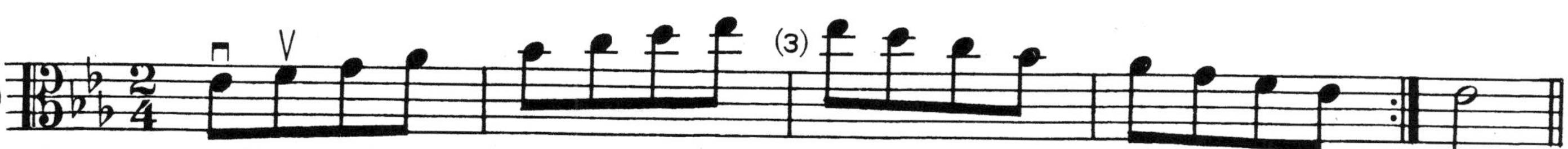

Also practice (1) slurring each TWO notes, and (2) slurring each FOUR notes.

Quarter and Eighth Notes

110 

111 

112 

Chromatic Scales

FIRST POSITION FINGERING

Ascending from open string: 0-1-1-2-2-3-4
Descending from fourth finger: 4-3-2-2-1-1-0

Also practice (1) slurring each TWO notes, and (2) slurring each FOUR notes.

113 

114 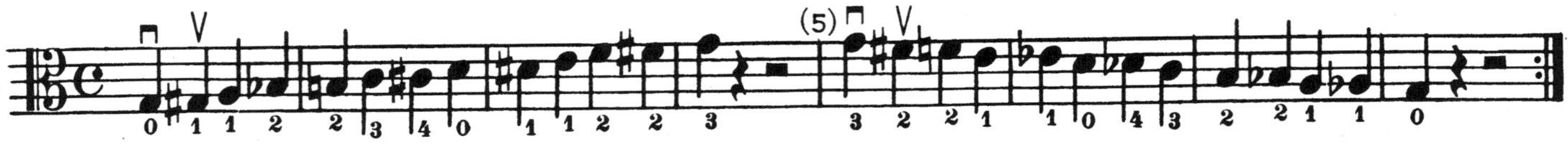

115 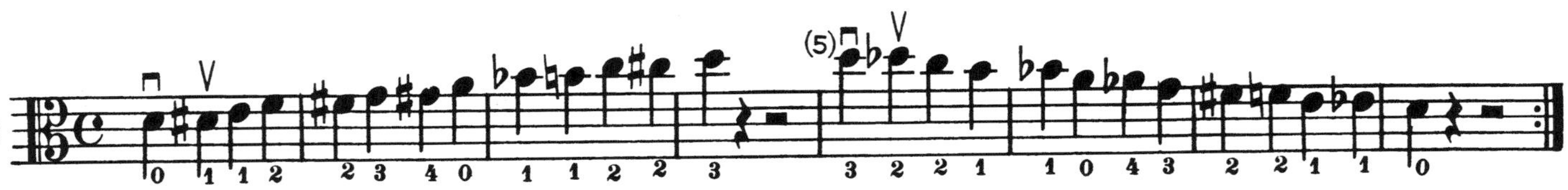

116 

117 

118 

119 

Extended Chromatic Scale

120 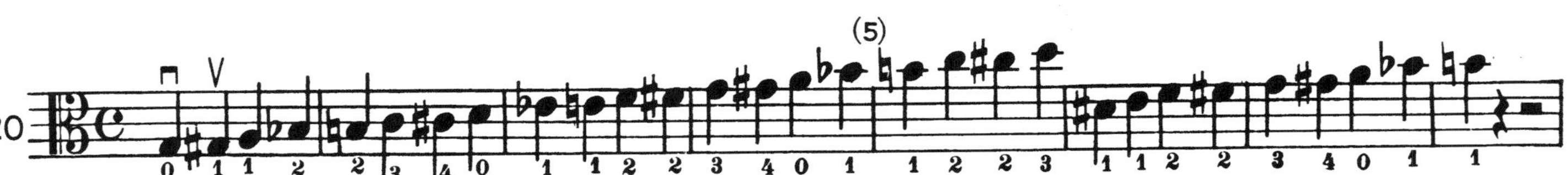

Also practice (1) slurring each TWO notes, and (2) slurring each FOUR notes.

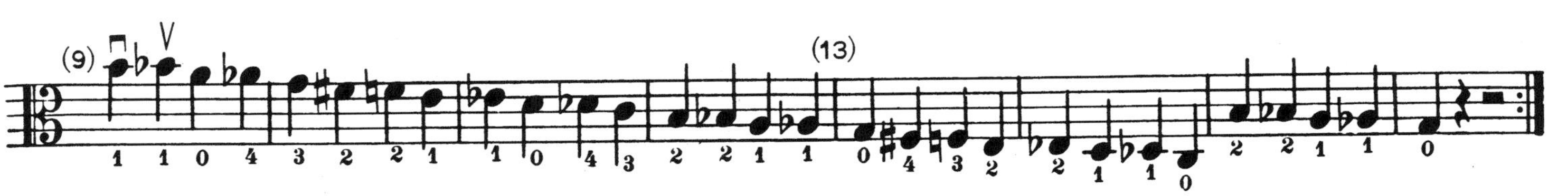